EMBERS IN THE ASHES

Embers in the Ashes

New Life in the Church

A "Pro-Vocation" for the Year of Faith 2012–2013

ABBOT MARTIN WERLEN, OSB

Paulist Press
New York / Mahwah, NJ

Cover image by Jean-Sébastien Charrière, OSB
Cover and book design by Lynn Else

Originally published in German as *Miteinander die Glut unter der Asche entdecken*

Library of Congress Cataloging-in-Publication Data

Werlen, Martin.
[Miteinander die Glut unter der Asche entdecken. English]
Embers in the ashes : new life in the church : a pro-vocation for the year of faith 2012-2013 / Abbot Martin Werlen.
pages cm.
"Originally published in German as Miteinander die Glut unter der Asche entdecken, 2012 by Kloster Einsiedeln, 6th Edition"—T.p. verso.
Includes bibliographical references.
ISBN 978-0-8091-4856-1 (alk. paper) — ISBN 978-1-58768-330-5
1. Church renewal—Catholic Church. I. Title.
BX1746.W4713 2013
282.09'051—dc23

2013012633

ISBN 978-0-8091-4856-1 (paperback)
ISBN 978-1-58768-330-5 (e-book)

Published by Paulist Press
997 Macarthur Boulevard
Mahwah, New Jersey 07430

www.paulistpress.com

Printed and bound in Canada

Contents

Foreword

When you drop a pebble into water, you know there will be ripples, but you can't foresee exactly how they will travel. And you don't want to. You don't want to spoil the excitement of discovery. You want to watch the ripples make their own way.

Abbot Martin Werlen has stirred the waters, trying to wake up the Catholic Church. He isn't giving directions. Mostly he is pointing out ironies and asking questions. After dropping the pebble, he is waiting and watching, and praying. He is, after all, a Benedictine monk, and that's what a contemplative mostly does, waits and watches and prays.

All of us who read the Bible are familiar with this style. Jesus did it with parables. He learned it from prophets and psalmists. All of them dropped pebbles that are still rippling and still waking us up just after we thought we were safely asleep.

Martin Werlen is not telling us what to do. He is offering us a chance to wake up.

Jerome Kodell, OSB
Abbot, New Subiaco Abbey
New Subiaco, Arkansas

Note to Readers

Embers in the Ashes has its origin in a talk given on October 21, 2012, by Martin Werlen, abbot of the Einsiedeln Monastery and member of Switzerland's Conference of Bishops, during a celebration commemorating the fiftieth anniversary of the Second Vatican Council and the opening of the Year of Faith.

Embers in the Ashes is a working document intended to provoke discussion and open to critique. Knowing that some readers are tempted to despair, we hope that this publication will encourage and engage many people to seek the embers in the ashes, so that together we may fan them again to fire.

1

The young man had every reason to expect that he would have a successful life. He was talented, surrounded by people who helped him advance, and he enjoyed a first-rate education in music: composition and violin. Everything pointed to his becoming a famous violinist. But often things do not turn out the way we wish. They wouldn't for this young man. At age eighteen, severe injuries from a car accident abruptly ended his career as a violinist.

It was sad. He had whatever was needed to become a successful musician: talent, fire, enthusiasm, support. But now in one moment all had vanished into an ash heap. It was not his fault; he hadn't been the driver.

All gone, many would lament. A pity! Regret, resignation. And he? Had he been rather narrow-minded, he might have kept trying with the violin. With a little bit of struggle, he might have been able to play well enough for the local orchestra, thinking, "Let's save what can be saved." Had he been more imaginative, he might have joined an action group engaged in working for greater street safety and advocacy for victims of accidents.

This young man chose neither of those paths. He faced his predicament. He tried to make the best of it. Under the ash heap, he discovered the remaining embers. Playing violin in top concerts had become impossible. But becoming a top conductor was a realistic goal he could pursue with unstinting dedication. Meanwhile the embers turned into fire. Today he is one of the top conductors in the world: Franz Welser-Möst, maestro of the Vienna State Opera.

2

Such examples are encouraging. Where there is much ash, there might still be embers that may erupt into a blaze anew. We must not forget that when thinking about the church. Many Christian women and men today mainly see ashes in the church. Pope Benedict XVI, too, was aware of it. On October 11, 2012, he proclaimed a Year of Faith. It was "to rediscover the joy of believing and the enthusiasm for communicating the faith."[1]

Not only Catholic women and men view—with deep regret—ashes in our church, but also people who belong to other faith communities or are wholly outside of them.

The thoughts offered here are to be a provocation. The term contains the word *vocation,* a call or calling. And the *pro-* clearly stresses that the calling is to be challenged and shaped in positive ways. These thoughts want to move things. They want to be a *pro-vocation*. They want to encourage our common search for the embers under the ashes so that the fire may burn again. Jesus Christ himself uses the image of fire in order to describe his mission: "I came to bring fire to the earth, and how I wish it were already kindled!" (Luke 12:49).

Let us face today's situation in the church and make the best of it: let the fire burn. Of course, we cannot address all questions, even the most important ones. If we were to attempt that, these lines would not move those who have settled in this world or in its way of thinking. And those who accept the ashes with resignation would lose courage to search further.

This text is not a catechism. That already exists. *Embers in the Ashes* seriously attempts to consider various criticisms. St. Benedict encourages it. In his Rule for Monks, he admonishes the abbot that if a guest makes any criticism, he should listen to it with prudence, since perhaps the Lord had sent this person just for this very purpose.[2] This is surprising—even today, some fifteen hundred years later. The directive is to be taken seriously. Is not St. Benedict the father of Western monasticism whose Rule has decisively influenced Western culture? Further, did not Pope Paul VI proclaim him patron saint of Europe in 1964? Did not Pope Benedict XVI intentionally choose him as his patron?

Those who systematically strive to silence the critics—not because problems have been solved—destroy the church, regardless of their pious pretensions. It is fatal if concerned baptized people are silenced simply because they call ashes by their name. We often hear the offensive comment: "If they don't like it, let them leave!" It is not the substance of the faith that bothers so many about the church, but what surrounds it. There are groups in the church among which everything the pope says or does may only be praised. In this, they are more pontifical than was Pope Benedict XVI himself, who wrote in the preface to *Jesus of Nazareth: From the Baptism in the Jordan to the Transfiguration*: "...it goes without saying that this book is in no way an exercise of the magisterium, but solely an expression of my personal search 'for the face of the Lord' (cf. Ps 27:8). Everyone is free, then, to contradict me. I would only ask my readers for that initial goodwill without which there can be no understanding."[3]

Critique is legitimate, indeed necessary, in the church. Sacred Scripture itself attests to it. Of course, not all critique will be considered here, nor will solutions to problems be offered. Nevertheless, encouragement shall be given to discover new, perhaps even obvious, ways, instead of falling into impotence, resignation, and helplessness. Some passages have been formulated pointedly to move things forward. They might also stir up dust. However, one can stir up dust only where there *is* dust. In addition, contradictions and dishonest patterns in the life of the church shall be mentioned—whenever possible with respect and love, and sometimes with tongue in cheek. To consider aspects of history may help us. But history is not simply the past. History is past, present, and future. Often history reveals why things are the way they are but also how they could be different today, even how they ought to be different.

Many things cannot be expressed in words. Most insights are gifts if we are not stuck on single words but ponder them, perhaps even meditate on them. The paintings of my confrere, Father Jean-Sébastien Charrière,[4] invite us to this: to face the piles of ash but not to get hung up on them, to seek the embers together, to start a warming fire together.

3

The old man whom the cardinals unexpectedly elected pope on October 28, 1958, saw a pile of ash. He had been quite a conservative ecclesiastic. But something else was far more important for John XXIII than his conservativism: his humanity, his Christianity. He viewed these as far more important than his predilections—whether of conservative or progressive origin. He was prepared to face the situation of the church and of the world. He was prepared to seek the embers under the ashes—the gift of faith—and to hand it on to the people of our time. He was prepared to listen to what God wanted to say today so that the fire would start up anew.

In many instances, the fire of faith could barely overcome the pile of ashes. Much had become cold and frozen over the ages. It still worked quite well because, in some European countries, the state had given various privileges to the church, and social pressure kept the institution together. For example, it was impossible for a baker's family not to go to church on Sunday. If the baker's family missed Mass, customers would have stayed away. Large numbers of people attending church, however, does not mean at all that the embers are the driving force behind attendance. So much was the way it was because it had always been that way. One simply had gotten used to it.

The violinmaker Martin Schleske points to the ashes that are hardly noticed in such situations: "It is a subtle form of unbelief if one has become used to what one believes.... In what one has become used to, the soul is without hope and the mind without question."[5] People of deep faith saw it in religious services, because much had grown cold and lifeless in the liturgy. One authority, discussing the liturgical reform in the wake of the Council of Trent, observed in the early 1960s: "The core of those measures consisted in centralizing all liturgical authority in the Sacred Congregation of Rites, the post-conciliar control organ that supervised putting the liturgical views of Trent into practice. Such a measure was double-edged, however. Proliferations were indeed avoided. But the fate of Western liturgy was now tied to a strictly centralistic and purely bureaucratic agency that completely missed out on historical sense and viewed liturgy purely as an issue of ceremonial rubrics, as a kind of courtly etiquette of the saints. Such an orientation implied an exclusively archeological understanding of liturgy that led from an exploring of vibrant history to a pure retention and therefore inner atrophy. Once and for all, liturgy had become sealed, a firmly encrusted set of forms that had lost the tie to concrete piety the more as one stressed the integrity of the prescribed forms....If divine services of the Church were to become again a divine service of the Church in its full meaning, that is, of all believers, it had to move on again."[6] This assessment is that of Joseph Ratzinger.

Old Pope John XXIII had been successful in bringing movement into the church. Nobody had expected it of him. The whole world was astonished. The movement also touched the Council delegates—against the strong opposition of some in the Roman Curia. It did not result from the Council delegates being either conservative or progressive but was embraced because they realized that more was at stake: a believable sign of our time. Fifty years ago, during the first days of the Second Vatican Council, the bishops assembled in Rome composed a message to the world that still today envisages the embers that they were seeking:

> To all people and all nations we want to send the message of salvation, of the love and peace that Jesus Christ, Son of the living God, has bestowed to the world and entrusted to the Church. We are therefore

assembled here on the wish of the Holy Father, Pope John XXIII....In this assembly, we want to find ways to renew ourselves by the guidance of the Holy Spirit, "in order to conform ever more faithfully to the gospel of Jesus Christ." We will strive to proclaim God's truth to the people of our time in its fullness and purity and in such a way that it may be understood and willingly accepted....Having come from all peoples under the sun, we carry the needs of the people entrusted to us in our hearts as well as their anxieties of body and soul, their pains, yearnings, and hopes. All the terrors that torment people also agonize our souls. Our first care belongs therefore to the poor and the weak. Following Christ's steps, we take pity on the many who are being tormented by hunger, misery and ignorance. We stand united with all those who are unable to lead a decent life because they do not receive proper help....[7]

That was the program of the Council that had just begun.That was the spirit of the Council from which the church is unable to distance itself without betraying its mission.

4

What about today, fifty years later? The situation is dramatic, and not only in German-speaking lands. It is dramatic not only because of the massive shortage of priests and religious but also because of the continued decline in church attendance. Such facts are easily determined. However, the real problem lies not in numbers. The real problem is that there is no fire! Those who want to praise or deplore the situation, citing numbers from other continents, remain stuck in the ashes. We need to face the situation and probe what lies behind it.

The numbers reveal many things. About forty percent of Swiss people belong to the Roman Catholic Church and about thirty percent to the Reformed Church. The third group, twenty percent, does not belong to any religion and is growing the fastest. Most of this third group or their families were once members of a Christian denomination. We need to think about that and act on it!

Should the decline continue, the scaled-down church and its institutions might indeed disappear in Europe. Those, however, who blame or even fight people of other religious groups, or those who have left a faith community, remain stuck in the ashes.

What should be done? People of a conservative bent try to salvage what they can. They look for allies. They celebrate the faith in small groups and lament the world's trends, especially its secularism and relativism. They blame the Second Vatican Council for the situation. The danger of such conservatism is that by holding on to the faith and admitting no change, it becomes distant from God, who wants to dwell among the people. It threatens to turn the church into a museum piece. This is precisely the temptation that the church resisted in the Second Vatican Council and its aftermath.

Progressively oriented people undertake and organize all kinds of programs in order to reach people. They take action in order to reach those in charge of the church. They seek to tackle the ash heaps by initiatives and concern for victims. The progressive danger lies in uncritically embracing change and thereby being swept away by modish trends. The church becomes superfluous. The Council has also withstood such a temptation.

Today the church is highly polarized between conservatives and progressives. This rift barely allows dialogue anymore. Often one side denies the other's ecclesial validity, that is, whether it is representative of the church. A look at the various media of the respective groups is alarming. One finds goodwill on both sides—at times only after a long search—and much ash. What is clear is this: if we as a church remain stuck in polarization, we prevent people finding the embers that mean life and must flare up again today.

Trench warfare does not promote enthusiasm. It separates. It cripples. The task of the church is not to support systems or positions of power. The temptation of wanting to preserve a system beleaguers conservatives as well as progressives. Only the labels look different. If we remain stuck in the old beaten paths, we contribute to the ash heaps. Furthermore, no one has charged the church either with shaping a parallel society or with total withdrawal. The great challenge—whether one thinks conservatively or progressively—is to avoid getting stuck in the dream of an ideal situation. An ideal situation has never existed.

Let us take the next step: the question in the church is not one of conservatism or progressivism. Nothing must remain the same because—from a human perspective—it has always been that way. Nothing must be changed because it is "in" to change everything. The task is being the church *today*, of taking charge *today*. It is a question of knowing the spirit of the times, to love the people of our time and to lead them to the gospel. The question is not to preserve formalities but to be faithful. We should not strive to be either conservative or progressive. Our concern must be to hear what God wants to tell us and then to do it. In this, we need the support of each other. As Blessed Pope John XXIII observed: "We are not on earth to look after a museum, but to take care of a garden in bloom."

This is the "other" path pointed out by the Second Vatican Council: to be a believer within change. This has nothing to do with conformity but much with the mystery of Christmas, the Incarnation. God becomes human in order to meet people where they are. We are able to take such an approach insofar as we are deeply rooted in faith and at the same time do not close ourselves off from the world. We must keep our ear on the heart of God and our hand on the pulse of time! It is our task to herald the gospel in the situation as given—today!—and to be the leaven in the world. The Council fathers took this attitude in dialogue with both those of conservative and those of progressive bent. If we simply look for passages in the Council documents that affirm our own position and overlook the wrangling and exchange from which they developed, we miss the core of the ecclesiastical event of the century. The Second Vatican Council showed a vibrant church in which the faithful were searching together.

Do people of our time, that is, a half-century later, view the church that way? In years past, many people in our country turned away from the church disappointed, whether by leaving it or—even more serious—by an inner distancing. People on an honest search—and today there are very many—wouldn't even think of turning to the church. Why? Where are the ashes that need to be discarded so that the embers may show clearly and a fire may rise again?

5

We need to ponder these questions seriously. Unfortunately that is what usually happens. There are ecclesiastics today who lament that, for forty years, the same problems are always brought up. This should not surprise anyone of average intelligence. The same problems are constantly discussed because they have not been resolved. Other ecclesiastics dare to assert that the problems were only those of German-speaking countries. This is, first, mostly wrong and, second, one must ask why problems in German-speaking countries should not be solved just because they might not exist among people speaking other languages. Problems need to be solved where they exist.

If we cannot address problems in such a way that encourages most of those grappling with them, we clearly fail to take the situation—as well as the people facing it—seriously. This also holds regarding the church. If problems are not being addressed or if one is not even to discuss them, one thereby compromises credibility—and, therefore, also faith itself. Essentials are at stake!

Not taking a situation or a person seriously is an act of disobedience. Because those in positions of responsibility do not realize their task and are, therefore, disobedient, understandable initiatives that are being started as emergency measures or as calls for help may lead to schism or the abandoning of an institution. Disobedience, lamented by officeholders, often results from the disobedience of those in office.

I can understand many initiatives that have been started in the past decades. But I myself would like—

together with the monastic communities at Fahr and Einsiedeln[8]—to try another path: to discover the embers in the ashes together. It is also manifest in readiness of facing and solving a problem on the spot. In this, we dialogue as much with the Swiss District Superior of the Fraternity of St. Pius X as we do with a well-known Tübingen theology professor. Is this the right path? At the September 2012 gathering of all Benedictine abbots in Rome—shortly before the synod of bishops devoted to the "new evangelization"—an abbot observed in his talk: "It is noteworthy to point out how little attention has been paid in the '*Lineamenta*' to the consecrated life." In this, too, we should not stop at complaining. If we look more closely, we discover indeed the significant absence of the religious in the preparatory paper, but perhaps it is a positive sign: a sign of our autonomy.

Let us look back. After Constantine issued the Edict of Milan in 313 (exactly seventeen hundred years ago), the church gained many privileges, such as, tax exemptions and state support that continue to this day. When these privileges are questioned or even being withdrawn, we assume that the church is collapsing. Our monasteries, too, benefit from these same privileges. We forget that monasticism originated as a protest movement against those very privileges. It was a prophetic movement, not in the state but in the church! From the start, monastic life has been an unexpectedly new, daring, living tradition.

At the time of the Reformation, the monasteries had long been without this prophetic power. We swam along with almost all the unsolved problems of the church. In that great crisis, one couldn't expect much from us, although it was precisely our vocation. We were concerned above all that everything would stay as it was—to our own material advantage. The important impulses that addressed the distress came from the new movements of the day.

If only monastic life was again a "pro-vocation," a prophetic sign in the church during the Year of Faith 2012–2013! We want to live in unity with the church, but not simply swim along in all its unsolved problems. Cardinal Kurt Koch,[9] our compatriot and president of the Pontifical Council for Promoting Christian Unity, argued in the words of Joseph Ratzinger: "A local church that wants to be Catholic without unity with Rome, would thereby lose its very Catholicity because a Catholicity that foregoes Rome is not Catholic any more. In turn, a local church that wants to be only 'Roman' would negate itself and merely turn into a sect, because a church that wants only to be Roman could not be Catholic anymore."[10] Simply stated, a local church that is merely Roman is as un-Catholic as a local church that is only anti-Roman. The same is also true for bishops. What is essential is to call ashes by their name so that we, as church, are not in the embers' way.

6

The disastrous assumption many people make of the church—and thus of its message—is: "Everything stays the same in the church." That impression is precisely the opposite of how people in the gospels reacted to Jesus. It is often said that he astonished them. The answers he gave to difficult questions and situations were not what they expected. Things didn't simply stay as they were. Jesus opened the eyes of people to new dimensions. He took them into a vastness until then unknown. Again and again, God gives us the gift, revealing unexpected ways leading into the future. The same is true of the saints. They didn't just do what everybody else did. They didn't stay with the old ways. Through the saints, God makes the gift of surprising ways that lead into the future. This confident optimism belongs to the rich tradition of the church. Do we see it today?

We need to avoid whatever deepens the impression of people: "Everything stays the same in the church." Of course, the issue is to preserve the full core of the faith. However, it always needs to show itself as new and surprising. That surely means that one has to leave era-specific externals and habits behind and to strive together with all—meaning all the baptized—toward finding the right path. A great contemporary theologian wrote: "There is on the one hand a way of thinking that proceeds from the full breath of the Christian tradition and, on that basis, tries to describe wide-ranging ecclesiastical possibilities; on the other hand, there is a purely system-bound way of thinking that allows only the present juridical form of the Church as the measure of its reflections and therefore must view any movement beyond it as a fall into the bottomless: Its conservatism rests on lacking historical awareness and on a want of tradition, that is a lacking openness for the whole of Christian history."[11] Again, this is Joseph Ratzinger speaking. Traditionalism is not an abundance of tradition; on the contrary, it is a dearth of tradition.

For instance, in traditionalist circles, altar boys still look like miniature clerics. (In Italian, the word *chiericetti*—little clerics—is still in use today.) This was understandable when liturgy was a divine service reserved for clerics. Only they could serve at the altar and were allowed a role in the liturgy. The altar was, of course, no place for women. What the choir was singing was not a valid part of the liturgy either. The priest had to repeat those texts quietly to himself. Only clerics performed the rites, if need be even small "clerics" as altar boys. Their attire, too, was consistent with this. The boys looked like little bishops, priests, or canons. Today altar girls and boys are dressed in white, symbolizing the baptismal robe. Having been baptized, they perform a liturgical service. The Second Vatican Council opened our eyes again to the treasure of our faith and tradition. This step has not been implemented everywhere. Even in St. Peter's in Rome, male "clerics," whether boys or men, are still serving—dressed as canons or like little bishops. It must at least give us pause today when priests celebrate the liturgy—without permission of their bishop—as if the Second Vatican Council had never happened. This example makes clear that it is not an issue of language.

It is important that we consider the rich tradition of our faith. Being knowledgeable about it helps us to pursue new ways without being suspect of modernism. Traditionalism makes people narrow-minded and rigid. Faith, however, gives scope. St. Benedict shared that conviction when he wrote: "But as we progress in this way of life and in faith, we shall run on the path of God's commandments, our hearts overflowing with the inexpressible delight of love."[12]

7

In recent years, the church has lost a great deal of credibility. It is clear that concrete witness in life is more important than mere words and texts. That many people equate church with pope, bishop, and priests, and perhaps religious, shows how little we live the insight that all who are baptized constitute the church. This becomes clear in pronouncements that should shock us. For instance, when ecclesiastics publicly claim that most sexual assaults do not occur in the church but in families, they reveal not only an irresponsible defensive attitude but also theological incompetence. They weaken the witness of the church. If sexual assaults occur in families of the baptized, they are just as much assaults within the church. All who are baptized constitute the church. The witness of all who are baptized is needed.

That witness is needed, as is the common search belonging to it. St. Benedict says that one had to determine carefully whether someone wanting to enter a monastery was truly seeking God.[13] People who already possess God are not wanted, but people who are seeking God. On September 2, 2012, in his sermon to a student group, Pope Benedict XVI alluded to it. The Catholic Church does not possess the truth. "No one can say: I have the truth—this is the objection raised—and, rightly so, no one can have the truth. It is the truth that possesses us, it is a living thing!"[14] It is significant how little such deep insight marks the daily life of the church. Should not the search for that truth be a common cause, a struggle that happens all over again in dialogue also, as exemplified in the Second Vatican Council? *YOUCAT*, the catechism for youth in the Catholic Church, was shaped in dialogue with young people.[15] In order to explore problems and challenges together, the German Conference of Bishops initiated a process of dialogue two years ago. Yet on his visit to Germany in September 2011, Pope Benedict XVI neither acknowledged nor encouraged such a process. Based on the rich tradition of our church, as well as the monastic rule of his patron saint, he could have given it some encouragement.

On September 16, 2012, a cardinal seriously asserted in a sermon preached at the assembly "Joy in the Faith" that met in Aschaffenburg, Germany: "In the gospel nothing is stated about dialogue."[16] Two years ago, Pope Benedict XVI made that aged cleric a cardinal and thus his close advisor. The claim of a man in such high position must prick our ears—as well as commentaries on an Internet message board that calls itself Catholic. In the tradition of the church, we read the gospel differently—and in communion with many saints. For St. Benedict, it is clear: if serious questions arise, all shall be called together because God reveals what is best quite often through the youngest.[17] Should less important issues have to be addressed, the abbot may consult only the older ones.[18] How might Pope Benedict assess the questions facing the church: important or less important? We cannot help but ask if the cardinal is perhaps reading a different gospel (see Gal 1:6ff.). In texts approved by the church, dialogue is referred to very often; even the word itself appears in the original text many times. For example, let us consider the mystery of the incarnation or the many talks of Jesus with people. Even our trinitarian understanding of God derives from a permanent dialogue within the divinity. All such understanding is given us by meditating on the good news as handed down by the church. However, cardinals do not appear in the gospels or in the catechism!

8

Based on the rich and tested tradition of the faith entrusted to us, the church has much to contribute to peoples' lives, for example, concerning human rights. But in this, too, it has lost its credibility for various reasons during the past years. The acceptance of a message does not depend primarily on its validity or intention but on how it is understood by those who are addressed. So-called "mixed messages" are especially disastrous: to assert one thing by words and say the opposite by deeds. Such behavior weakens the testimony. As true as the words might be, they will be barely noticed. Such a mixed message is perceived concerning the church's position on human rights. Time and again, people say the church supports human rights but takes no interest in them within its own ranks. Such an observation is simply denied most of the time.

St. Benedict would probably say, if someone offers a critique, one should carefully consider whether the Lord sent such a person precisely because there's an issue. If the church took such a position, it would gain much credibility—also regarding human rights. Some church groups that seldom enjoy the full support of leading ecclesiastics are annoyed when the church takes a stand on human rights that they don't like. An example is the treatment of asylum seekers. How can we defend an attitude of contempt or indifference toward people who flee from other countries, when Jesus himself identified with those in need? This could become the counter witness of our time. "I was a stranger and you welcomed/did not welcome me" (Matt 25:35, 43). This must not leave us unconcerned. Blessed John Paul II made this striking comment on Matthew 25:35–36: "This Gospel text is not a simple invitation to charity: it is a page of Christology which sheds a ray of light on the mystery of Christ. By these words, no less than by the orthodoxy of her doctrine, the Church measures her fidelity as the Bride of Christ."[19]

St. Benedict begins his monastic rule with the admonition "Listen!" In our time, many people do not view the church as a listening church—listening to God and the people God loves. Only as a listening church will we be able to answer the distress of people—when we become aware of their distress and meet them as God meets them.

9

Today the church—let's face it, the world-church—is driving with the brakes on. This makes being engaged in the church less than attractive. Can the radius of action be large without becoming unfaithful to the Jesus message? On the contrary: precise faithfulness to the Jesus message demands courageous action. If we are committed to what has been entrusted to us, we will pursue it with all available means and make it known. Then we will leave behind defensiveness and start a liberated and liberating offensive. A church, dedicated to the preaching of the gospel in our present time, doesn't need super-people in the dioceses and monasteries but people—trusting God's presence—who face life with courage.

Many believers point to situations that need to be addressed. The problems are known. Pope Benedict mentioned them on occasion. But barely anything concrete is being done about solving them. Numerous solutions have been presented out of deep faith, love for people, and love for the church—by theologians who are today in the highest offices of the church. But the proposals are being ignored by those in authority.

Let us think, for instance, of the treatment of people whose marriages have failed and who live in new relationships. In this regard, the Roman Catholic Church has never repudiated the solution followed by the Orthodox Church. We could learn much from the experience of our Orthodox sisters and brothers and find a way that would allow us to be leaven for people whose path has not been ideal. It is they who especially need to experience the reality of the church as a healing force.

Courageous steps into the future are missing. Vision is missing. Creativity is missing. The highest places in the church have promoted ecclesiastical groups that are fearful of courageous steps into the future. Does this reveal the power of faith? St. Benedict admonishes the abbot that he has rather to provide than to preside.[20] Does this not apply to all who hold sacred office? Felix Gmür, the bishop of Basel, Switzerland, points in that direction in his statement of October 16, 2012, made at the Synod of Bishops in Rome: "And when a Christian makes a proposal or offers a criticism, are we listening with sincerity? The monastic rule of Saint Benedict admonishes the abbot in this matter: 'The abbot should prudently consider whether the Lord has sent him precisely because of it' (RB 61, 4). I think that we need to listen more and to discern with good will what Christians tell us."[21]

Even small steps could help regain much credibility for the church. In this, one could fall back on the best apostolic tradition. One could also take important steps in the ecumenical union with the Eastern Church and in healing the split in the West. To that, the rediscovery of synodal processes also belong. If institutions, such as, synods of bishops are being prepared for and monitored to such a degree that nothing new can emerge, does this show trust? Should what happened in the Second Vatican Council not also occur here: bishops being conscious of their responsibility and facing change—with the help of eminent women and men who are theologians—and in unity with the pope? And for God's sake, let well-meant papers be just vehicles for sharing ideas!

10

During the last decades, the appointments of bishops have destroyed much of the church's credibility. In the twenty-first century, the baptized and confirmed people of a diocese should routinely be involved in the selection process for bishops. The church reminds us of this often: it is astonishing what St. John Chrysostom (+407) writes about the election of Matthias in his commentary to the Acts: "As the fiery spirit to whom the flock was entrusted by Christ and as the leader in the band of the apostles, Peter always took the initiative in speaking: 'My brothers, we must choose from among our number.' He left the decision to the whole body, at once augmenting the honor of those elected and avoiding any suspicion of partiality. For such great occasions can easily lead to trouble. Did not Peter then have the right to make the choice himself? Certainly he had the right, but he did not want to give the appearance of showing special favor to anyone. And it is reported further: 'They nominated two men: Josef, called Barsabbas with the epithet Justus, and Matthias'....He himself did not nominate them; all present did."[22]

What did the church mean when it inserted this text into the breviary for the Feast of St. Matthias? It probably means that we are to consider it and to draw our own conclusion. But can the church forbid it in fact without thereby losing much credibility? Certainly, participation in choosing a bishop might fail—but hardly more than today's process in the selection of all bishops. In religious orders, the democratic choice has remained the custom for centuries and has generally been a success. The present abbot of Einsiedeln was chosen in conformity with St. Benedict's Rule (of the sixth century!), and his election was confirmed by Pope John Paul II. It was at least no obstacle for the latter's beatification.

11

The celibate way of life is as much a possible way of following Jesus as is the conjugal one. Both are charisms—God's gifts. Among the baptized, this is hardly understood anymore. We have managed to present the following of Christ in celibate chastity in such a way that it is seen simply as a law. Canon law declares: "Clerics must observe perfect and perpetual abstinence for the sake of God's kingdom; they are therefore obligated to celibacy as a special gift of God by which the spiritual officeholders become attached to Christ with an undivided heart and thus may devote themselves more freely to the service of God and the people."[23] Could it not be phrased differently? Could not the admission to ordination be expressed in another way and thus the celibate way of life of Christian women and men be understood differently? For instance: "The celibacy of clerics, chosen for the kingdom of God and fitting for the office of priest, is to be valued highly according to the tradition of the Universal Church. The status of clerics who live the married life should be honored likewise in conformity with the practice of the Primitive Church and the Eastern Communities."[24]

Progressive-minded baptized people might shake their heads and say this is impossible. It is far too removed from Rome's mentality. Conservative-minded baptized people might suspect the author of heresy, as they had thought all along. Both sides may be surprised when they realize that the proposed text is an official text of Rome, signed by the beatified Pope John Paul II. It is the canon 373 of the canon law for the Eastern Churches that are in full communion with Rome.

This shows that other ways are possible. Whoever immediately assumes heresy should ponder what it means to be faithful to the pope. Clearly, no issues of faith are involved. The issue is being faithful to one's calling, and the faithfulness of the church to its task. Canon law needs to be in the service of that faithfulness. Everything should be done from this perspective: "Having the salvation of souls in mind: that must remain the supreme law in the Church."[25] In ecclesiastical history, therefore, canon law has been questioned and, when proper, adapted anew. These are not changes undertaken because others have been making them, too, or rejecting them because it had always been that way. What is at issue is living our vocation in tune with today.

12

God affirms humans. The church must strive to join that affirmation all over again with all its heart. Humans are men or women. The church finds it difficult to say yes to women. In the question of sex, the church appears awkward and clueless. Cautious steps are a special edition of the *Osservatore Romano* that is shaped only by women every fourth Thursday and the employment of some women to implement tasks at the Roman Curia, something unimaginable only a few decades ago. Such gestures are welcome but also rather embarrassing. We may mention that although Pope John Paul II decided in 1992 to allow women to perform the tasks of altar boys, this was only made public in 1994. What holds for people in leading positions also applies to officials of the church: to miss decisions at the proper moment may damage a cause. It is embarrassing. But a matter will not improve if one simply denies it. It has to be dealt with.

As mentioned before, cardinals do not belong to the essence of the faith. In this, too, there could be much latitude for new ways. The pope's advisory board could look different. For instance, people from all over the world, women and men, young and old, could be chosen for such a board to serve for five years. Every three months, they would meet with the pope in Rome. None of the participants would say or withhold something out of career concerns. These meetings could bring a different dynamism to church governance. Questions of greater and lesser importance could be addressed.

An Austrian journalist expressed this opinion about the Vatican that many share with her: "A petty group of schemers."[26] That weakens the charge of the church and the credibility of its witness far more than insiders realize. The pope suffers; the whole church suffers. Whoever has the power to change such a system also carries the responsibility.

Because of destructive events at court, there was a jester among the courtiers. He held a court appointment with the necessary freedom to put unpleasant facts on the table or to offer criticism. In the church, an analogous institution is missing. On occasion, engaged Christian women and men would tackle it, and because of the high regard in which the faithful held them, later popes canonized them. Those who think these thoughts are heretical must have read the wrong gospel (see Gal 1:6ff.). As already said, neither the gospel nor the catechism mention cardinals, but Jesus' clear injunction: "It is not so among you" (Mark 10:43; CCC 1551).

In the 1994 missive *Ordinatio Sacerdotalis*, Pope John Paul II affirmed that priestly ordination is reserved for men and declared the question beyond discussion. Yet the question remains: is a person's gender a matter of faith? Does it belong to the immutable core of the faith? At least after 1994 we can still discuss this even more basic question. A glance at tradition is surprising also in relation to this issue. In order to remain faithful to its mission, the church has created new positions. For instance, consider the introduction of the diaconate (see Acts 6:17). Over the centuries, the church has referred to spiritual fatherhood, but rarely—and today hardly at all—to spiritual motherhood. This is understandable considering that for centuries the guild of theologians almost exclusively consisted of men. But it is also surprising. The gospel speaks explicitly of spiritual motherhood but not of spiritual fatherhood. "Whoever does the will of God is my brother and sister and mother" (Mark

3:35). The question is not one of sexual identity but of the imitation of Christ. A Christ-centered approach prevents us from becoming captives of culturally shaped and theologically defended patriarchal structures. Reorienting ourselves to the Bible and the whole tradition may help us to find our way out of culturally shaped restrictions.

13

Many people view the church as an institution that doesn't serve life but limits life. For many—even for those who are baptized—it has become irrelevant. Whether or not this impression is justified, it is certainly widely shared. Surely it is legitimate for such people to expect that the church will help them to discover him who promises life in fullness (John 10:10). The primary concern shouldn't be about what the church is *against*, as is often perceived, but what it is *for*, where its voice is often seen as missing. The musical conductor, referred to in the beginning pages, who did not get stuck in the ashes, mentioned his distance from the official church in an interview. But when asked of what Austria could be proud, he mentioned two ecclesiastics: "Recently I got to know Father Georg Sporschill. It is marvelous what he is accomplishing in Moldavia for the poorest of the poor, how he digs deep into the pockets of the well-to-do also deserves recognition. He as well as Bishop Erwin Kräutler are people who are impressive and deserve high esteem; they could sit comfortably here in Austria in a monastery or in a rectory."[27]

To the Jesuit Father Georg Sporschill, we owe the noteworthy interview about the situation of the church that

Cardinal Carlo Maria Martini granted him shortly before the cardinal's death. The cardinal observed: "Father Karl Rahner liked using the image of the embers that are to be found under the ashes. I see so much of the ashes that lie on the embers in the church that I am sometimes tormented by hopelessness." He demanded that all in the church turn around: "The church—starting with pope and bishops—must acknowledge mistakes and take a radical path toward change....For two hundred years the church has stagnated." Change must not happen in the embers (the core of the faith) but in that which has become ashes. From there, surprising shifts follow: "The question should be reversed from whether the divorced may take communion to this: how may the church, by the strength of the sacraments, come to the assistance of those whose marital relationship is in crisis or has failed?"[28] In this, a person does not stop at the ash heap or turn away disappointed. Cardinal Martini wants the church to rediscover the embers and allow people to experience them.

14

The reactions to the plain remarks of Cardinal Martini differed widely. On the Internet, he was even accused of heresy—precisely by people who insist that nothing said by the pope can be questioned. But it is not that simple. Pope Benedict XVI was aware of what kind of person, Christian, and bishop he was talking about. In his message for Cardinal Martini's funeral, Benedict wrote: "He was a man of God who not only studied Sacred Scripture but loved it intensely. He made it the light of his life....And for this very reason he was able to teach believers and those in search of the truth that the only Word worth listening to, accepting and obeying is God's, because it points out to everyone the path of truth and love. He was such with great openness of mind, never refused to meet and converse with anyone....He was such with a profound spirit of pastoral charity, according to his episcopal motto: *Pro veritate adversa diligere*—attentive to all situations, especially those that were more difficult, lovingly close to those who strayed, who were in a situation of poverty or suffering."[29]

At the end of the interview, Cardinal Martini asked the interviewer a counterquestion: "What can *you* do for the church?" The question pertains to us all. We all are the church! Let us sally forth anew and seek the embers under the ashes together. Thus the "Year of Faith" becomes truly a year of faith. And the fire may burn anew.

15

"Synod 72" was the 1972–75 synod of bishops held in Switzerland in order to implement the decisions of the Second Vatican Council. From that synod resulted the four prayers for special concerns—basically originating in the monasteries of Einsiedeln and Fahr. Today the prayers are in the Roman Missal of the Roman Catholic Church and have spread all over the world in translation.[30] The prayer, "Jesus Our Way," asks for the spirit from which the gift of the Second Vatican Council derives. A sign of hope!

JESUS OUR WAY

Merciful God,
by taking part in this celebration
grant us the Spirit that fills us with life.
Renew us in the image of your son.
Strengthen our oneness with all your people,
with our Pope N. and our Bishop N.,
and with all women and men
called to serve the church.
Let the faithful understand the signs of the times
and use all their power for the gospel.
Open us to what troubles people
so that we share with them their grief and fear,
their joy and hope,
and as faithful witnesses of the Good News
go with them to meet you.

Notes

1. Benedict XVI, *Porta Fidei* (2011), n 7.

2. See the Rule of Saint Benedict (hereafter RB) 61,4. The translation used is *RB 1980: The Rule of St. Benedict in English*, ed. Timothy Fry, OSB (Collegeville, MN: Liturgical Press, 1981).

3. Benedict XVI, *Jesus of Nazareth: From the Baptism in the Jordan to the Transfiguration* (New York: Doubleday, 2007), xxiii–xxiv.

4. Artist and monk of the abbey of Einsiedeln.

5. Martin Schleske, *Der Klang. Vom unerhörten Sinn des Lebens* (Munich: Kösel, 2012), 16ff.

6. Joseph Ratzinger, *Ergebnisse und Probleme der dritten Konzilsperiode* (Cologne: J. P. Bachem, 1965), 18ff, 20.

7. www.konzilsblog.ch, October 20, 2012.

8. Einsiedeln Abbey is a monastery of monks and Fahr Abbey is a monastery of nuns in Switzerland, both part of the Benedictine Confederation. Together they form a double monastery, one of the few in existence today, with the abbot of Einsiedeln ruling both communities.

9. Kurt Koch (b. 1950), Bishop Emeritus of Basel, Switzerland.

10. Kurt Koch, *Die Kirche Gottes. Gemeinschaft im Geheimnis des Glaubens* (Ausgburg: Sankt Ulrich Verlag, 2007), 266.

11. Ratzinger, *Ergebnisse und Probleme*, 61.

12. RB, Prol, 49.

13. See RB 58, 7.

14. http://www.vatican.va/holy_father/benedict_xvi/homilies/2012/documents/hf_ben-xvi_hom_20120902_ratzinger-schuelerkreis_en.html (accessed March 11, 2013).

15. Michael J. Miller and Benedict XVI, *YOUCAT: Youth Catechism of the Catholic Church* (San Francisco: Ignatius Press, 2011).

16. Cardinal Walter Brandmüller, September 16, 2012.

17. See RB 3, 3.

18. See RB 3, 12.

19. John Paul II, *Novo millenio ineunte* (2001), n. 49.

20. See RB 64, 8.

21. http://www.kipa-apic.ch/?na=0,0,0,0,d&ki=236470&pw=BKf8_ogJ.

22. Homily III on the Acts of the Apostles.

23. *Codex Iuris Canonici* (Rome 1983), Can. 277, 1.

24. *Codex Canonum Ecclesiarum Orientalium* (Rome 1992), Can. 373.

25. *Codex Iuris Canonici* (Rome 1983), Can. 1752.

26. http://www.kipa-apic.ch/?na=0,0,0,0,d&ki=236456&pw=ovF*KdZ2.

27. http://www.kleinezeitung.at/nachrichten/kultur/2611255/japan-man-fast-gottaehnlich.story.

28. A translation of the entire interview can be found at http://ncronline.org/blogs/ncr-today/translated-final-interview-martini (accessed March 21, 2013).

29. http://www.vatican.va/holy_father/benedict_xvi/messages/pont-messages/2012/documents/hf_ben-xvi_mes_20120903_card-martini_en.html (accessed March 11, 2013).

30. A revised version of this prayer is part of the Eucharistic Prayer for Use in Masses for Various Needs III in the *Roman Missal* (Third Typical Edition).